THE CROSS AND THE SPIRIT

1

THE CROSS AND THE SPIRIT

BY

H. C. G. MOULE, D.D.
BISHOP OF DURHAM

WIPF & STOCK · Eugene, Oregon

Wipf and Stock Publishers
199 W 8th Ave, Suite 3
Eugene, OR 97401

The Cross and the Spirit
By Moule, Handley C.G.
ISBN 13: 978-1-60608-950-7
Publication date 7/24/2009
Previously published by Pickering & Inglis Ltd., 1898

Contents

I

The Galatians

IN considering the Epistle to the Galatians attention must first be given to the people to whom it was addressed, the conditions that called it forth, and the teaching of the Epistle as a whole.

1. *Its Recipients*, who had responded to the Gospel preached by St. Paul, were those of a large highland district of Asia Minor. These were now scattered in several mission stations, not massed in a large centre; they formed (1. 2) "the Churches of Galatia." As to race, they were an amalgam more or less complete; a Phrygian substratum, with inserted Greek and Roman and Jewish elements; all affected and dominated by a Celtic population, the conquerors of the region about two centuries and a half before. These were the Galatæ, sons of the great Celtic family, poured into Asia Minor when the return-waves of the primeval migration westward rolled eastward, first upon Italy, later upon Greece, and now upon the land of the Phrygians. True Celts, they were noble specimens of man in point of ardour, and the enthusiasm of religion and of affection; but their risk lay in the lack of persistence under common and chronic trial.

Among them St. Paul had spent some time, a time longer than he had planned, for the stay was due to an illness (4. 13), "on account of weakness of the flesh," that is, somewhat obviously here, "illness of body." It was an illness, perhaps, connected with the mysterious "thorn for the flesh"; for he speaks of it in the next words, if we adopt a very probable reading, as "*your* temptation in my flesh;" as if in its nature it were a trouble which would dispose them to think him, not merely a sufferer, but emphatically not a favourite of heaven. But they had not yielded to the temptation. They had "received him as an angel of God," nay, as the Redeeming Lord Himself. They had infinitely "congratulated" themselves on their new joy and glory. They were ready to dig out their eyes and give them to the beloved missionary. He on his part had been permitted to impart to them the fulness of Gospel blessing; he had set forth before them with amazing vividness the glory and work of the Crucified; "Jesus Christ had been painted large upon His cross, to their very eyes" (3. 1). And Paul had been to them the instrument of a rich effusion of the Holy Ghost, poured out, according to the promise, from the ascended Lord. They had "inaugurated their Christian life in the Spirit" (3. 5). This was in the sense, partially (so it would seem), of a manifestation of miracle such as that which marked to so extraordinary a degree the Mission at Corinth. But far more, surely, in Galatia as at Corinth, it was in the sense of that supernatural fulness of divine life, the life of love, joy, peace, and spiritual power, which is at once the highest and the most permanent evidence of the saving and sanctifying baptism of the Spirit.

These were the two outstanding phenomena of the evangelization of Galatia; the prominence of the atoning Cross and the fulness of the Holy Spirit. And by a necessary consequence the whole spiritual character of the Galatian Mission was profoundly and consciously connected with an immediate hold by faith on the Saviour Himself. For what was, and always is, the supreme work of the Eternal Spirit? Not to generate a new and separate Gospel as if we were to advance from the School of the Son into that of the Spirit. No; He is given above all things that He may glorify Christ. There is no token of the Spirit's mysterious fulness present in our hearts so sure as this, that Christ becomes to us in hallowed consciousness our all in all. The Apostle might paint Christ large before the very eyes of the Galatians. But it would need the fulness of the Spirit in their hearts to make the picture live, to make the Son of God in His dying and rising glory a transfiguring reality to their being. But so it had been. They had begun in the Spirit.

2. It was into this happy scene of life and gladness that *an alien propaganda* now intruded itself. I shall not attempt at any length to discuss the ideas and watchwords of Judaic Christianity; it would be necessary if I did so to take up among other things the difficult question of its varieties of type and phase; the phenomenon as it was at Colossæ compared with what it was in Galatia. All that I think needful for our present purpose is to remember certain obvious features of the school as a whole. First, it was not ever explicitly, perhaps not consciously, anti-Christian, in the sense of denying the Messiahship of the Lord Jesus. In that respect it lay and it worked within, not without, the Church. But then in theory and in practice it minimized Him, and it tended to neutralize Him. It affirmed pertinaciously the permanence among the vitals of salvation of large parts, at least, of the Mosaic covenant and its institutions. It made Moses the porch to the temple Christ, always and for all. The safety of the soul was suspended in an important measure upon the acceptance of circumcision and the observance of the calendar of the Law; probably also upon just such connection with the institutions of the priesthood and the altar as was possible to Jews of the Dispersion generally. In short, the man who would be saved must become a proselyte in order to have a true position as a convert; he

could not touch the hem of the garment of the Lord except within the curtains of the Tabernacle.

It is more than probable—we may say, looking at the history of the Church, it is certain—that these Judaists, these early anti-Paulinists, tended in their belief to very inadequate views of the Christ Himself. When we come to the Ebionism which is so much connected with their school this appears in an extreme form. And in the New Testament itself we have only to consult the Epistle to the Colossians to see from the line of its argument that the errors with which it deals had much to do with a minimizing creed of the Person of the Son of God. The magnificent passage in Colossians I., one of the very greatest of the apostolic utterances upon His eternal and universal glory, can hardly be understood aright except as an assertion of truth which was ignored, which was undermined, if not contradicted. But even had it been otherwise theoretically, and no doubt with many Judaists it was so, it would be inevitable that the system as a whole should practically minimize Christ Jesus to the spiritual sight and consciousness of its disciples. For it came in upon an evangelization in which He had been the Alpha and the Omega, and undertook to supply its defects and guard against its errors. Obviously *the stress* of the new message would lie somewhere else than upon the glory of Christ in Himself, and the magnificent fulness of His redeeming work, and the divine simplicity of His call, "Come unto Me, believe in Me." The new preachers would gravitate another way for their themes and appeals. Even if no word were ever spoken by them depreciatory of the eternal greatness of Jesus Christ, their message would not be primarily of Him. It would deal with circumcision, and the ceremonial code, and the virtues of the great days of the Calendar, rather than with what Christ is, and what He has done, and is doing, and is coming back to do. He would not be banished from the system, but by no means would He be really set upon its throne.

It would be somewhat as it fared with the Sun in the system of Ptolemy. The glorious orb was, of course, provided for, in place and sphere, in the old cosmogony; but he was only the most brilliant and powerful of the moving bodies which circled around Earth as their centre. But Christ, in the true system of the Gospel, is the Copernican Sun. He is the immovable Centre, glorious and supreme; the Lord and Sovereign of the whole moving order, its source of light and source of life; "in all things having the pre-eminence."

I may be allowed to pause here for a passing remark. There is a Judaist element, may we not say, in every human heart. For where is the heart that, even religiously inclined, puts Jesus Christ into His wonderful right place in its inmost creed, by nature? In our ministration of the Gospel, let us remember this. I am strongly persuaded that we take it far too much for granted that habitual worshippers and habitual communicants see Christ aright (I mean in doctrine, in theory), see the personal and ever blessed Lord, in His incarnate, sacrificed, risen, living, coming glory, as "all their salvation." We do well to instruct them or to remind them, according to occasion and as far as there is time, in truths of the second order. But nothing, literally nothing, must be permitted to minimize our treatment of the supreme things, of the supreme Thing, the Lord Jesus Christ Himself. It is as true as ever that "the natural man receiveth not the things of the Spirit of God, for they are foolishness, folly, unto him; they are spiritually discerned." Our duty is not to forget this, and accordingly to lay ourselves out to be, if He pleases, His vehicles for His own spiritual teaching, by making the supreme truths of the supernatural Gospel the supreme thing in our ministry of the Word. They need all the emphasis we can give them.

In Richard Cecil's fragmentary writings, a storehouse of truth and suggestion, there is a passage to this purpose. It touches on the illustration just given from the Ptolemaic and Copernican systems. Take a totally uneducated man, he says, and set yourself to convince him of the truth of the true system of the universe; to make him perfectly sure, against all the evidence of sight, and all the usages of human language, that the sun is stationary to the earth, and that the earth is one of the minor globes which roll round the sun as their imperial centre. You will not find your task easy. You will need line upon line, and explanation upon explanation. You are aiming at nothing short of a mental revolution. Even so it is, says Cecil, with the true preaching of the true Christ. The minister of the great mystery of blessing needs to remember that in more instances than he can guess he has to aim at being the vehicle, under God, of both a mental and spiritual revolution. He has, so far as he may, to show the mighty reasonableness of the affirmation that Christ is, for us sinners, all and in all. He has to speak so that he may ask his Lord to take the words and use them not only for the illumination of the reason, but for the glorification of Christ to the heart as the Sun and Centre of everything; Lord, Life, Way, End; Righteousness, Sanctication, Redemption; Pardon, and Holiness, and Heaven.

I will not apologize for this excursion from

our main road. The matter is not irrelevant, though it lies on an off-line. But now I return to the more immediate subject, the Epistle to the Galatians itself. We have remembered in outline who the recipients of the Epistle were, and their characteristics and their spiritual history; in particular, the fact that in their evangelization the two mighty factors of the glory of Christ and of the power of the Spirit had been supreme: We have reviewed briefly and simply the nature of the alien propaganda which disturbed them, and which occasioned the Epistle. It has been apparent that the radical error of that propaganda, in St. Paul's view, was just this, that it minimized Christ to them. It put the secondary first, and the primary second. It drew them down to second causes, and to a spiritual life at second hand. Accordingly his intense desire is to write to them so as to redress the awfully disturbed balance; to remind them with all the energy he can of Christ their whole salvation and the Holy Spirit all their power; to paint Christ Jesus again large upon the Cross before their eyes, and to dilate again on the overcoming and delivering power of the Spirit in their hearts, received by faith, evidenced in pure and happy holiness. Incidentally he has much else to say. He has to assert his own authenticity as a real messenger from God, supernaturally informed and accredited.   He has to illustrate this by incidents of biography; by the facts alike of his independence of the other Apostles and of his intercourse with them.   He has to speak with tender severity of the moral as well as spiritual mischiefs into which the Galatians were drifting; speculative error working itself out into unhallowed tempers; "ye bite and devour one another."   He has to denounce in plain terms the immediate author of the deplorable change. But all these things lie as accessories around the main theme, the double theme which twines itself always into one—Christ and the Spirit.

II

The Galatian Epistle

A PARAPHRASE-OUTLINE of the contents of the Epistle, intended to serve in some measure as a running commentary, is offered herewith.

CHAPTER I

PAUL, divinely commissioned Apostle of the Risen Jesus Christ, greets, along with his Christian companions, the mission-churches of Galatia, in the name of the Father and of His atoning Son our Lord, who died for us, to set us free from the power of a sinful world. I hear with distress that you are lightly drifting from Christ's grace to alien beliefs; beliefs which, because alien from His true glory, cannot possibly be true. Woe to the propagandists of them; woe to me, woe to angels, should I, should they, preach anything as a substitute for the grace of Christ. For myself, I am absolutely unable to modify my message; I should not be Christ's bond-servant if I did. It is not my invention; it is my commission; I cannot modify it for man, nor plead for any modification of it from God.

But be you assured that the message you have

2   17

heard from me was out-and-out divine, authentic
from the throne. It was not even learnt by
me from other and original apostles; the Risen
Lord personally unveiled it to me. You will
remember my story; my advanced Jewish
studies, and creed, and persecuting Jewish zeal.
But then came the hour of grace, the inward
revelation to me of the Son of God, that I might
henceforth preach Him to the nations. And
that crisis was followed not by consultation
with mortal brethren ("flesh and blood") but
first by a retirement in Arabia; then by a return
to Damascus; then, after an interval of three full
years, by a visit—a fortnight's visit—to Peter,
including an interview with James the Less.
Then came life and work for a long time at
Antioch, and in Cilicia, so that mine was practically an unknown face in the missions of Judea.

CHAPTER II

FOURTEEN years thus passed, and I visited
Jerusalem again, with Barnabas, and with the
once pagan Titus. I went, obedient to a divine
intimation, in order to compare my message
with that of the elder Apostles, and so to assure
myself whether or no there was aught lacking
in my Gospel, intended by the Lord to be
supplied by them, and without which supply
my efforts would be more or less a failure. But
there proved to be nothing of the kind. As to

usages and rites, not even Titus, prominent as
his position was, and weighty therefore as his
case would be as a precedent, was compelled
by the Jerusalem Apostles to accept circumcision. The recognised pillars of the mother-
church added nothing to me; said nothing to
imply that my truth was not the whole truth.
A cordial arrangement for the division of labour
between me and the three, headed by Peter,
was the main result of the meeting; so little was
I, so little was my Gospel, discredited by them,
the alleged patrons of the new teachers in
Galatia.

True, there was a time when Peter visited
Antioch (that first great scene of Gentile
Christianization), and unhappily wavered there
in his line of action, under Judaistic pressure;
even Barnabas was swayed for a while in the
same direction. But I openly challenged the
conduct of my great elder brother. I reproved
him, on the express ground that our acceptance
with God is secured not by a ceremonial dis-
cipline but by faith in Christ; by that acceptance
of Him and reliance on Him which identifies us
with Him in His atoning death and in His risen
life. In that life now we live, even here below,
divinely free and victorious. To go back from
this is to return to bondage; it is to return by
our own act to unpardoned guilt, it is to re-
constitute *ourselves* transgressors.

CHAPTER III

Now let me come direct to your present case. What has happened to you, after so glorious a beginning—to you, to whom Christ was so vividly presented, the Spirit so richly given in response to your simple faith? Is not your whole experience against the change? Does the *new* Gospel bring, as the old did, the Spirit's hallowing and wonder-working power?

Do you want authentic precedent for the distinctive message of my Gospel? You have it in Abraham himself. He received all his vast blessing not as a ceremonialist but as a believer; not by law but by faith. Would you be his heirs indeed? Then take his way to claim the inheritance.

Alas for us, otherwise! The awful, inexorable Law has no promise for the sinner; its very nature is to sentence him to death. It was precisely because of this that the Lord died. Against us ran the death-warrant; and He bought us out from it. He bore our sins, in the sense of taking their sentence on His head, that we might—not only be forgiven, but be Abraham's heirs of amplest blessing, receiving the promise of nothing less than the Spirit, through faith.

And all this is provided for in the very Scriptures of the Law. Before they tell us of the Law, the Covenant of Sanai, they tell us of a

free promise,, the Covenant of Grace with
Abraham (and with his seed, his single line of
covenant inheritance, the line of Isaac only,
which line is embodied and summed up in
Christ). The Scriptures place between the
two Covenants a broad gulf of time, four full
centuries, in order to bring the lesson home;
as if to say that the eternal antecedent Grace
could not really be meant to be abrogated by
the long subsequent Code of precepts taken as
conditions of blessing.

Yet that Code *had* its sacred work. It was,
for one thing, a practical curb on transgressions.
It was also, and more deeply, a means to conviction of sin and need; "concluding all under
sin"; pending the time when the glorious Seed
should come to claim the free grace for us. ·

Notice, further, another difference—the Law
was mediatized, conveyed through Moses, who
stood as a third between two contracting par-
ties, God and us. But the Promise was simply
given, given sovereignly from Him, the ONE
Personage in the great act. Without desert,
without claim, without goodness on our part,
He gave His CHRIST to us.

Thus the whole inmost purport of the preceptive Law (moral as well as ceremonial) was
to school us up to a sense of our need of Christ,
in order that, accepting Him, we might be
accepted in Him, just as we are. So, in that

respect, our days of nonage are over; we have entered on our position and our property. Faith, pure and simple, places us among the very children of the Eternal. Our baptism, the symbol, seal, and sacred outward counter-part of our faith, identifies us with His Son who died for us, and robes us as it were in Him. As thus identified with Him, we are one with one another; all barriers of rank, race, and sex are fused in Him; we are lawful heirs together of Abraham's blessing.

CHAPTER IV

THERE was indeed a time, even our unenlight-ened past, when we were in the slave-like position of pupilage. But the destined crisis came, and with it came the Incarnate SON, Woman-born, perfect Keeper of the Law and therefore perfect Redeemer of us law-breakers, in order now to secure our lawful adoption as God's own children in Him. And then with Him came (you *know* it *has* come!) that blessed gift, the SPIRIT of the Son, crying out in your hearts, *Abba*, *Father*, to the Father of your Lord. The work wrought for you, the work wrought in you—all combines to say, "Child of God, heir of God, live thy glorious sonship out."

Alas, why are you drifting now away from such eternal truth and hope? What means this almost return to old idolatries? This salvation by calendars and types? Is all the happy toil of evangelization in vain? I entreat you to be as I now am; for I once stood where you now are. I implore you to remember the first dear days of conversion; your love and tender sympathy for me when ill and prostrate; your joy, your glad congratulation, your undreamt-of wealth, discovered now in Christ. Are you afraid of me now, because I tell you the old truth? Are the new missionaries able to separate me and you so soon—all for their own ends? Ah, be both more stable and more warm than this. I am in travail with you again, in my longing to see not ceremonialism but CHRIST take shape in you. Oh that I could be again amongst you, and speak with a living voice; but with a voice of warning now.

But once more; are you so anxious to go back to the Mosaic order? Then listen to a deep parable, divinely planned, taken from the Mosaic books. You remember Ishmael and Isaac; Hagar's son, born in bondage, Sarah's son, born in freedom, and heir to the great inheritance. Here is spiritual teaching. Hagar is Sinai (that hill of wild Arabia, the land never associated with Israel's joys); and her child is Man—man as bound by the violated Law; type of such as they are now who cling to the earthly Jerusalem, and her temple, and her altar.

Sarah is the heavenly Jerusalem, the holy commonwealth of God's redeemed in Christ, of every tribe and tongue.   Once she was a barren wife, while the pagan world was unvisited by the Gospel; now she is as fertile as she is glorious. Her sons are we; the Isaac of the better Covenant, children and heirs of God in Christ.

Remember by the way the action of Ishmael upon Isaac; his cruel, mocking jealousy.   Here too is parable.   The false claimant to heirship still hates, mocks, persecutes the true; so let me not wonder, and do not you wonder, if the would-be Mosaist, with his days and months and years, turns fiercely upon you who meet him only with Jesus Christ, and nothing of your own.   What is this but another evidence that you are the children of the free?   It is but the prelude to the exclusion of the slave-born from the home.

CHAPTER V

THEN hold your freedom fast.   It may seem a light thing to add circumcision to the Gospel. But no; your circumcision will mean for you nothing less than the acceptance of the whole awful legal responsibility.   It will mean your saying, "I am now bound *to do*, to do in the Law's sense, that I *may live*."   That means self-salvation; and self-salvation means despair.   It means, letting go the magnificent rest and power of grace; Christ for you, Christ in you.

Our true position is just this; justified in the Christ whom we receive by faith, filled with the Spirit whom we receive by faith, we look for that blessed hope, "the hope of righteousness," the coming glory of the justified; and this is still, by faith—that is to say, through Christ accepted, through Christ relied on as our own. In Him, this is all; circumcision, non-circumcision, those differences are *nil* in Him. The one question is faith, a living reliance, made manifest in love.

Once more, whence has come this change over you? Not from the God who converted you. Some minute but permeating influence of evil is at work; an individual is your leaven. I am sure that you will come to your right mind; but great is *his* guilt meantime. Do your new teachers say that I too after all preach circumcision (because I caused Timothy to be circumcised)? My reply is very practical. Why, if it is so, do they thus track my steps and thwart my work? Forsooth the Lord's Cross, His atoning, liberating death, has ceased to be a stumbling-block to them, if they claim me as their sympathizer!

I could wish that your troublers, with their Gospel of circumcision, would cut themselves off from us wholly, so truly pagan is their whole conception,

For indeed, brethren, it is to a divine liberty
that you were called in your conversion; only,
a liberty which is not selfish licence but the
love which loves to serve, loving others as the
self; and *that* is the spiritual essence of the Law.
Take care of the dreadful opposite condition
and temper promoted by this false Gospel. It
is showing itself too plainly; you are quarrelling
already; you will ruin each other soon.

What then is the antidote to it all? It is
just this, the HOLY GHOST, received, obeyed,
and used. Live in His light and power, and
you *shall* be emancipated from the cravings of
the self-life (see verses 19-21), the flesh. The
two powers are both present with you, antagonists eternally, the self apart from God, and
the Spirit of life and power; a counter-agency
continually affecting will and action. Give
yourselves to the Spirit's leading, and you shall
not be under the Law; you shall be *in* it, you
shall be *with* it, loving the will of God from the
heart, but you shall not be *under* it, as Damocles
was under the sword.

You know the works of the self-life; look
around you—are there none of them in view?
Impurity, idolatry, wizard tamperings with the
unseen, hatred and envy, bloodshed, and de-
bauchery, these are they—things which shut
men out for ever, as you know, from part and
lot in the kingdom of God.

And you know, too, the fruit, the sweet, perfect product, of the power of the Holy Ghost in a believing heart; love, joy, peace, long-suffering, gentleness, goodness, fidelity, meekness, self-control. The Law is quite at peace with such lives. Now if you belong to Christ, you have left the self-life on His Cross, condemned and executed. *It* cost the Lord His death; what have you to do with His murderer? If you live by the Spirit, who has joined you to the Lord, see that each step of conduct is governed by Him too. In His power, for you *can* do it in His power, drop the miserable self-spirit, the vanity, the envy, and walk in love.

CHAPTER VI

ONE word to those who may say, "But we *are* spiritual, we renounce these legalisms, we know only Christ and the Spirit; we are good and faithful Paulinists!" Is it so? Then prove it by the work of the divine Spirit; of *meekness* towards the brother who, you think, has fallen from truth; you are weak enough yourselves, apart from that Spirit whom you theoretically assert. Take another's burthen up (if you *are* so strong); bear it for him, in the sense of sympathy. Do not be self-deceived, as if *you* were great and good; you are nothing—it is all the Lord. Remember, your freedom is not irresponsibility; every individual has his own load of sacred duties, and he must give account about it for himself to his Master.

Among other burthen-bearings, support by your willing gifts your pastors, your faithful teachers.

Remember the law of spiritual results; God is not to be imposed upon. No true Gospel ever means real licence to conscience. The self-life and the Spirit-life are both sowings; each has its infallible harvest. Let us think with joy of the Spirit's harvest-home; live out His life in you, in watchful, unselfish, helping love, especially to Christian brethren; and we shall reap indeed.

What large letters I have penned my message in! I was resolved to write an *autograph*.

Once more—the teachers who say, "You must be circumcised," are men who want to stand well with their own world, which world cannot bear the doctrine of the atoning Cross and its full salvation. They are not real Mosaists themselves; *I* can say that with authority, for I know what full Mosaism means in its tremendous reality. They want your names, a list of so many external converts to glory in. But God forbid that I should glory in anything. but in the atoning Cross of our Lord Jesus Christ. There, clasping it, nailed as it were to it, in union with Him, it matters little to me how I stand with my world, or any world. In

Him, the one question is, not circumcision or uncircumcision, not a list of Judaists or Paulinists, but a new creation, lives born again to HIM.   Peace and mercy on all who go by that rule; they are the true Israel, God's own chosen, princes and priests to Him.

Now to close.   I claim henceforth a right to have heard the last of this opposition among you.   Why?   Because I am a lord and autocrat?   No, but because I am a slave.   My body bears, in many a scar, the brand of my Master, Jesus.   And my Gospel is not mine, it is His; I am absolutely nothing but His messenger.

Brethren, His grace, His living peace and power, be with your spirit.   Amen.

The Doctrine of Christ

WHAT does the Epistle say to us about the blessed Name of our Lord Jesus Christ?

We notice first the general fact that the Name appears everywhere. The Epistle contains 149 verses. In these there are at least 45 explicit mentions of our Lord Jesus; that is, one for every three or four verses on an average. And these figures give an imperfect impression; for many of the mentions are such that they not only mark points but cover surfaces, running out into statements about the Lord which can again be subdivided into others. This alone is nobly significant, this ubiquity of Christ in the texture of the Epistle. And I hardly need remind you how characteristic it is not of the Epistle to the Galatians only but of the New Testament Scriptures generally. As we read them with that suggestion in our minds, we shall indeed receive an ever-deepening impression that Christianity is in fact Jesus Christ; the Lord is His own Gospel; Subject-matter even more than Teacher.

Coming to details, we find some hints here, and we find such hints more fully in many other places of the Epistles, of the human biography of the Lord.   We find Him (4. 4), "when the fulness of time was come"—when the ideal occasion had arrived, foretold and prepared, and He was "sent forth" by the Father, evidently from a pre-existent glory—we find Him "becoming, born, of woman."   Here is an allusion which certainly does not of itself inform us of the virginity of His sacred Mother, but equally certainly falls in with it.   And the next phrase there, "come to be under law," indicates not only His human but His Israelite parentage; as, of course, does also 3. 16, where the Christ is the "seed of Abraham"; so, too, 3. 29, "if ye belong to Christ, ye are Abraham's seed."   This, however, is a point almost superfluous, as it is already obviously implied in the term "Christ" itself.   Then we have repeated allusions to the fact of His Death; that word so familiar to us that we, and our hearers, only too often fail to realize its abiding mystery and glory.   Assuredly no *à priori* and imagined Gospel, conceiving, if it could do so, of a holy Incarnation, would have gone on to make the grand sequel of that Incarnation to be—not a life of splendid and omnipotent achievement, but a death of violence, shame, and indescribable distress.   Yet this is just what the true Gospel does.   It utterly denies us leave to contemplate the Incarnation out of spiritual reference, in its first regard, to the Cross and Passion.   So here we have the incarnate Lord dying (2. 21), "If by law is righteousness, Christ *died* for nothing." And His death is crucifixion: 2. 20. "I have been nailed to the *Cross* with Christ"; 5. 11, "the stumbling-block of the *Cross*"; 6. 12, "persecution with reference to the *Cross* of Christ"; 6. 14, "exultation in the *Cross* of our Lord Jesus Christ, by means of which (or, of whom) to me the world has been crucified, and I have been crucified to the world." Then, consequent on the Death, is the Resurrection; 1. 1, "God the Father raised Him from the dead": 2. 20, "Christ in me liveth."

One detail of His biography seems slight in itself, but it has manifold importance as we consider it. Quite incidentally, in a purely narrative statement of his own action, St. Paul mentions his having seen (1. 19), "James, the brother of the Lord." It is as simple and natural a mention as if he had said, "I saw Timothy," or "I saw Sergius Paulus." But think for a moment what it suggests; the re-cency, and the absolute reality of the human biography of the Christ. Not now to discuss the question of what the "brotherhood" was between James and the Lord, it was *some* purely human relationship, whether of blood or of convention, which might just as well have sub-sisted between other two Palestinian men. As such, the allusion carries us far up beyond the

natural range of myth and legend; it places us at
once where we can hold intercourse with people
who were not only contemporaries of Jesus, but
shared a home with Him, and were classed and
ranked with Him in human life.   Placed immediately beside allusions to the eternal and
divine side of His existence, how striking this
is!   As we shall see immediately, St. Paul pours
out, all over the Epistle, allusions to this same
Person which assign, to say the least of it, a
superhuman character and power to Him.
Quite passingly and naturally he speaks of Him
as, concurrently with the Eternal Father, send-
ing down "grace and peace" upon the human
soul; as being the ultimate and inmost secret of
all spiritual life for the world.   Yet also he was
just James' Brother.   May we not say with
reasonable confidence, with a faith which feels
fact beneath its steps, that this astonishing
collocation, so calm, so unexcited, so unforced,
one limb of it stated in just the same fact-like
tone as the other, can be explained only by
fact?   Is not this entirely unlike the manner of
invention, conscious or unconscious?   Written
down within thirty years of the Crucifixion
(and how luminous a retrospect is thirty years to
a man in middle life!) this reference to the
family of Nazareth, made without an effort, in
the same breath with adoring references to the
divine operations and prerogatives of a Member

3

of that family, makes material for much thankful
and reassuring thought.

But we turn now more directly to the asser-
tions of the superhuman, the divine, aspect of
Jesus Christ and His work. We find Him first,
then, to be more than man: for (1. 1) Paul is
"an Apostle *not* by means of *men*, but by means
of Jesus Christ." Again (1. 12), Paul received
and was taught "his Gospel" *not* as "transmitted
by man, but by Jesus Christ's unveiling," *i.e.,*
as the context assures us, by means of an unveiling of truth effected by Jesus Christ. More
explicitly still, we find Him "the Son of God,"
and so designated in connexions which fully
justify us in saying that the phrase implies a
Filiation which means part and lot in the eternal
Nature: 1. 15, "It pleased God to unveil His
Son in me," as a mystery needing the Infinite
Hand to lift its veil, and let it shine into the
depths of the human soul for its salvation.
Again, 2. 20, "What I live in the flesh, I live
in, under the condition and surroundings of,
my faith in, my reliance on, the Son of God."
Again, 4. 4, "God sent out" (as from the recess
of the eternal Presence) "His Son, made of a
woman." So before us shines that fair and
wonderful light of the Gospel, the eternal Sonship of Him who is also born of woman. It is
not only (if "only" may be reverently said in
such a connexion) that GOD becomes man; it

is the SON of God.   And the words carry with
them, let us note, not only an announcement of
wonder and glory, but an insight into the very
heart of divine love.   I know not if it is with
others commonly as it is with me; but I must
confess for myself, with humble thankfulness,
a peculiar power upon faith and love in just this
word, "the Son of God," when I ponder it in
connexion with the question of personal salvation.   It carries with it, to the believing
sinner, a supreme guarantee of welcome to the
heart of the FATHER.   It reveals to me something of the internal love of God for God, and
then it carries down to me, in the Christ, incarnate, sacrificed and glorified, nothing less
than that very love.   I am in the Son; what
must I not be to the Father?

   This great Son of God appears in the Epistle
in the exercise of many functions.   He is the
autocratic Master of His follower; Paul is
"Christ's bondman" (1. 10); he "bears in his
body the servile brand of the Lord Jesus"; he
is shown by the scars of persecution to be not
a self-reliant hero but the bought property of
his Redeemer (6. 17).   Christ's disciples are
"His," belonging to Him: "If ye are Christ's"
(3. 29): "They that are Christ's" (5. 24).   On
the other hand, He is such to them that, as we
have seen, being His bondmen they are also,
equally, wonderfully, sons of God in Him the

Son: 3. 26, "You are all God's sons by means of
your faith in Christ Jesus": 4. 4, 5, "God sent
forth His Son that we might get (as our intended
portion), our filial adoption." And 4. 7, "So
thou art no more a bondman but a son, and if a
son, an heir." Such again is this wonderful
Christ that His redeemed are not only in His
possession, or under His protection; they are
"in Him"; words significant of a union profound
and vital, illustrated elsewhere by the imagery
of the Head and Limbs, which is here only
implied. The Churches in Judea are "in
Christ," 1. 22. All believers are "one" as it
were one compound *personality*, because their
Head is one (3. 28). "In Him" is the sphere
where faith works by means of love (v. 6).
Those who are baptized in His name are "clothed
with Him," involved in Him (3. 27). "In Him"
resides our justification (2. 17), as much as to
say, we must be in Him to get the acceptance
which He has won for us, "In Him" His ser-
vants have a sacred liberty (2. 4).

And all this blessing for us has been dearly
won for us by Him in whom we are so richly
to enjoy it. All through the Epistle, as we
have already seen in part, runs this red line of
atoning and redeeming Passion (1. 4), "He gave
Himself as a sacrifice for our sins that He might
take us out of this present age so evil." He
lifts us, as it were, above its grasp, so that we

are in it and not in it, kept from its evil while
enabled in face of it to walk with God; free in
the profound peace of the pardon He has won,
and in the inward power of the Spirit which also
is ours because He died in order to.pour the
gift of Pentecost upon. us. Would we enjoy
that life of emancipation, and live "in the flesh"
(2. 20) yet as "taken out of the world so evil"?
It must be by faith in Him, not as He appears in
any of His characteristics but specially in *this*,
that "He loved me, and gave Himself over on
my behalf" (2. 20). Would we estimate the
awfulness and the love of His dying work aright?
We are to remember that when He died (3. 13),
"Christ bought us out from the curse, the death-
warrant, of the law, becoming on our behalf a
curse" (tremendous words, which would have
been denounced as a parody on truth if they were
not as a fact found in Scripture); "for it stands
written, Accursed is every one who is hung on
tree." Nothing short of this was the condition
precedent to our receiving the blessing of
Abraham, and the promise of the Spirit.

We note, by the way, how unconscious
Scripture is of the repugnance of some of its
interpreters to a so-called "commercial theory
of salvation." Twice over does St. Paul here
use the words translated "He bought out"
(3. 13; 4. 5). For him, such is the Lord's
dying work in expiation and in satisfaction, that

from one great side it not only *can*, it *must*, be
imaged by the transactions of the market-
place; the paying down by Him of infinitely valu-
able consideration that we, altogether on that
account, may be released. And the party to
whom here the consideration is paid down is
surely the Law, violated by us, satisfied by Him
for us. In other words, the mystery of His
Passion and Death had reference to the awful
claims of eternal Holiness with its categorical
commands. It dealt so with them that we,
because of that Passion, and because of it alone
in the sphere of legal righteousness, find the
grasp of the Law's arrest and bondage upon us
relaxed, and walk out free.

Let us not forget further that the imagery
points on its other side to that sacred bondage
which alone is perfect freedom. For what
does it say? Not, "He *delivered* us" (as indeed
He did), but, "He *bought us out*." Our release
is so effected that by the very act we are ac-
quired, appropriated, possessed. "Not your
own, for you were bought for value." "Whether
we live therefore or die, we *belong to* the Lord."

This process of our deliverance by the Son
of God is put before us, again, in this Epistle
as our Justification. See 2. 16, "Knowing that
man does not get justification in consequence
of works of law, but only by means of faith in
Jesus Christ, we too believed in Jesus Christ,

that we might be justified in consequence of
faith in Christ . . . . But if, seeking to be justified in Christ, etc." And again, 3. 11, "That
in law no one gets justification before God,
is evident; because 'The just in consequence of
faith shall live.'" And again, 3. 24: "The law
was our pædagogus up to Christ, that we might
be justified in consequence of faith." And
again, 5. 4: "You disconnected yourselves from
Christ, such of you as are getting justification
in law; from grace you fell. For we by the
Spirit, in consequence of faith, are looking out
for the hope of righteousness." If I at all understand these last pregnant words, they mean that
we are looking out, with an expectation sure
and certain, for future glory, as the issue of
"righteousness," namely, of our acceptance for
Christ's sake, our justification in Him. Of
course I have regard in this interpretation to the
large context of St. Paul's language elsewhere,
especially in the Roman Epistle (see *e.g.*,
Rom. 3. 21-24). But I think this is amply
enough to secure the interpretation, in view of
the *context* of Galatians 5. 5. He is thinking
here not of our condition, but of our position;
the Lord's winning for His people this wonderful "extradition" to Him, from under the curse
of the Law, into the smile and sunshine of re-
conciliation with the Lawgiver. There they
stand, His purchased property, His much more

than amnestied, His welcomed and acclaimed, members and brethren; embraced for His sake, and in union with His person (see 2. 17). And standing there, on the ground where penitent reliance is their foothold, they look up from thence, and, in the same reliance, see the Gate Beautiful from the Hills Delectable, rejoicing, as the justified, in "hope" of glory.   For "whom He justified, them He also glorified."

It is almost needless to point out that, as in the more extended discourses of Romans, so in these briefer lines, we have the word *dikaioun* used in its only proper reference.   It has to do with law, and tribunal, and a sentence proclaiming that the law is satisfied, and that the accused is accepted by the Lawgiver.   "To justify" is a word (we need continually to re-member this and to explain it) not of internal condition but of relative position.   It denotes not our subjective amendment or cleansing, in the region of will, but our objective acquittal, in the region of law.   Only the acquittal is more than acquittal, for it is welcome, it is acceptance. So complete and magnificent is the reason why, the procuring cause, the price paid, the glory of the substituted Sin-bearer, that the sentence of the law, through the lips of the Lawgiver, upon those who (considered in themselves) merited only its "curse," is not merely, "You may go."   It is, "You must come."   It is a welcome to the embraces of the Judge, and to adoption into His wonderful home.

Very instructive, by the way, is the manner in which in this Epistle the two conceptions of Justification and Adoption are never confused, but—collocated and treated in living relation. Perfectly separable in idea, they are profoundly connected in spiritual fact. And their *nexus* is our Lord Jesus Christ, and our union with Him by faith. He is at once the Son of God and the Sin-bearer for man. And the benefit for us of both His two characters is appropriated and realized by faith. And faith's revealed efficacy is that it puts us into union with Him, in all He is for us. As we are guilty, it puts us into union with Him who has perfectly satisfied eternal Law as our Representative. But we are also aliens, and He is also the beloved Son. Therefore it also puts us into union with Him in filiation. And so the affiance which receives from the Judge the gift of His more than acquittal receives also, in the same act, from the Father, the gift of His adoption into sonship.

Only in the briefest way need I point out the practical import of the words "faith" and "believe" in all this connexion. Assuredly their great outstanding idea is reliance, affiance, the taking the Trustworthy One at His word. The whole purport of the Epistle leads that way, to say nothing now of the ample proof of such a reference from our Lord's own use, always, of the words *pistis* and *pisteuein* in the sense of personal trust. From one view-point then "faith" is the simplest thing in the world; and happy the soul which remembers this, and acts upon it, in life and in death. From other sides it is the most profound and pregnant thing in the world. As exercised by a sinner in view of His Redeemer crucified and glorified, what does it not connote? It is by its very act a confession of self-condemnation and self-aban-donment; and it is by its very act a confession of the glory and all-sufficiency of Jesus Christ. It repudiates utterly all moral merit in itself. By its very nature, faith looks out from and forgets itself; it is occupied with its Object. Salvation by faith is salvation wholly by Christ trusted.

In closing this section of our Studies, I note in passing a detail or two in the Apostle's doc-trine of Christ.

v. 1, "Christ made us free"; He is the Liber-ator obviously from the bondage of condemna-tion, the internal slavery of the unforgiven and alienated. On the other hand, He is the Law-giver; 6. 2, "Fulfil the law of Christ." His liberty is on the other side order and loyalty; His freedmen are also, from the point of view of His blessed will and rights, His subjects, aye, His bondmen. Only, His law is now not only the categorical precept, but the formative power.

Lastly, 4. 19: "Till Christ take shape in you." Here is formative power indeed; and it is not an abstraction but a Person. This wonderful Christ, so absolutely One in Himself, so multifarious in His function for us, appears here as living and moving in His disciple, who on the other part lives and moves in Him. He is "Christ, which is our life." And the moral and spiritual development of the Christian is accordingly expressed in this wonderful term, of the development of Christ in him. The Indweller is there, and as it were grows in His dwelling, and fills it more and more. And so the plastic dwelling takes His shape. "The life of Jesus is manifest in the mortal flesh."

IV

The Doctrine of the Spirit

I HAVE by no means exhausted the references to our blessed Lord's Person and work in the Epistle, but enough has been said to suggest a deeper study of a theme always inexhaustible in itself. A few words therefore upon the doctrine of THE SPIRIT in the Epistle.

Here again, as in our study of the doctrine of the Son, we begin by remembering how ample is the material. It is not indeed by any means so great in quantity, but it is very considerable, in point of mere mentions. And the mentions, as I said above on the other group of texts, very often not only mark points, but cover surfaces; affecting a whole context.

The spiritual lesson of this is deeply important. The Galatian Epistle is on the whole very prominently an Epistle of Justification. Like its great sister-Epistle, Romans, it lays extraordinary emphasis on ideas of guilt and its removal; law, curse of the law, expiation, justification. But is it therefore a *merely* "forensic" tractate? No, like Romans again, it has all along, or at least all underneath, another supreme theme, which is in a sense its ultimate theme. It has the doctrine of the Eternal

Spirit.   Our justification, in the inspired teaching of the Apostles, is no *mere* legal arrangement terminating in itself, or terminating at best in a conception of mere safety.   It is indeed a sublimely legal arrangement, and is indeed God's own method for our blessed safety.   But it stands related all the while to something else, as foundation is related to Temple, or as porch to Church.   We are justified *that we may be inwardly sanctified*.   We are accepted that we may, at peace with God through Christ *for* us, receive from God the Spirit who shall make Christ a power *in* us.   The justified man who has not the powerful presence of the Spirit in him is a sorrowful anomaly in the idea of the Gospel.   For large illustration, see the Roman Epistle, where the majestic argument leads us to our awful sinfulness first, then to our Propitiation, then to our contact with Him in His death, by faith, then to our union with Him in His life, and then, in the climax of the eighth chapter, to the richness, the exuberance, of our possession in Him of the Holy Ghost in all His grace and power, making "Christ in us" to be our all in all for life and holiness.

In Galatians, the sacred Spirit is before us (4. 6) as "the Spirit of *the Son* of God"; unspeakably connected with Him in being and in operation.   Those who are Christ's "live by the Spirit" (5. 25), *i.e.*, in view of the context, it is by the Spirit that they possess the eternal life as principle and power; born again by the Spirit, out of nature into grace.   And by the Spirit also (*ibidem*) they are called to "walk," *stoikhein*, "to take *the steps*" of real life; using their possession for their practice, meeting each temptation and each duty with the *recollected* resource of the Holy Ghost given unto them.   "By the Spirit" they are to give themselves to be "led" (5. 18), away from self and its will, into and along the will of God.   There is present in them always the mysterious "flesh" (5. 17), the self-life in at least its latent possibilites of manifold evil.   But then (*ibidem*) there is present in them also the Spirit; not here the spirit of man but the Spirit of God; a positive power antagonistic to the flesh.   Let them yield themselves to the Spirit, let them "walk by the Spirit" (v. 16), and the Spirit of God shall deal with the self-life as their best and highest efforts apart from the Spirit can never do.   Yielding themselves thus to the Spirit, they will produce "the fruit of the Spirit" (v. 22, 23), the whole harmonious product, sweet to God and man, of a life supernatural in source yet beautifully natural in development.   Their life of obedience will thus be a "sowing to the Spirit" (6. 8)—as it were a casting upon the soil of His presence in them the seed of acts of regenerate love, to bear the harvest hereafter of the "Well done, good and faithful." Would they, in ever fuller measure, "receive the promise of the Spirit"? They are to do so "by faith" (3. 14); relying as simply upon God's faithfulness for *this* gift as for the gift of pardon and acceptance; even as the Lord said (John 7. 39), "He that believeth in Me, out of his belly shall flow rivers of living water; and this spake He of the Spirit, which they that believe on Him should receive."

Meantime this wonderful Gift is not necessarily reserved for late and distant stages of Christian life. Nay, the convert is to possess and enjoy it from the first; "Ye did *inaugurate* your life by the Spirit" (3. 3). And yet the gift, ever needed, was always ready to be continuously given again, from the eternal springs of God; God is (3. 5) "the continual Supplier of the Spirit." In Galatia, that supply, we gather, was often accompanied and attested by "miracles" in the accepted sense, marvels of abnormal operation on matter as well as spirit. Yet the stress of the thought of the Epistle is far more upon the purely spiritual miracle of a life really transfigured in Christ. "The spiritual man" must show his endowment mainly by the sweet "fruit of the Spirit," and not least by the Spirit evidenced in the *meekness* of the Christian.

Detached Passages

"FOR I through law died to law, in order to
live to God" (to *enter on* life to Him)
(2. 19-21). With Christ I have been, and am,
crucified. But I am alive; not *I* any longer;
there lives in me Christ. Such life as I do now
live in flesh, in faith I live it, faith in (of) the
Son of God, who loved me and gave Himself
over on my behalf. I do not nullify (almost,
stultify) the grace of God. For if through law
is righteousness, then for nothing Christ died."
He died when there was no need for His death;
He threw His death away.

We have here one of the great passages of the
Bible. A full treatment is impossible in this
space; but a little may be said in detail on some
main points.

(*a*) "I through law died to law." Here, as
in the Epistle to the Romans, "law" means the
divine preceptive code, taken as a condition of
salvation; "this do and live." "Law" does indeed often, in the light of context, mean the
Mosaic institutes. But even then the word
has regard to its larger idea; those institutes
were a particular specimen of the universal fact
of law in the sense just given. Now to "law,"

so understood, how did Paul "die"? Certainly
not in the sense of becoming callous to its
precepts. No; it is in the sense of entirely
renouncing his hope of salvation in the law's
way. As it were, he fell down dead at Sinai,
pierced with the conviction that "the law was
spiritual, he was carnal." He ought to keep it
all; he could not, in the sense of the divine
demand, keep it at all. It said, "Thou must
die." And that sentence his own conscience
at last fully echoed; he died subjectively, as one
who owned his sentence just, and who now
must seek life elsewhere if he was not to sink
for ever. Then came the Lord, with His death,
His death under the law's sentence, His wonderful death, the issue of which is life to all who
are found in Him. And Paul, invited to His
side, flies there, and is joined to Him. Now
in another sense again he "dies to law." For
the Lord has "died to it," satisfying it by His
sacrifice, rising from His grave eternally at
peace with it, for Himself and His. Paul has
now therefore, *in Christ*, suffered the stroke of
death, and in Christ is risen to the joy of re-
surrection-life. He is now "living to God,"
related now in all his happy being to this God
of love, this God of Christ.

Law thus "killed" him, first, in his inner
experience, as to self-righteous hopes. Law,
further, carried out its death-sentence on him,

4

when it sentenced his blessed "Sin-Bearer" to the Cross. Now accordingly he is dead, first, to his old hopes, for he is a convinced sinner; and also, further, to his old fears, for he is a penitent believer. And in the light of the love of God he now "lives" indeed to him, in His Son.

(b) "I have been, and am, on the Cross with Christ." Here are words which put with inspired vividness and power the fact of the believer's identification with his Saviour, in the vicarious suffering of the Head for the limb. He died for me, suspended on the Tree of shame and expiation. And I am joined to Him; so there I also died. By no "legal fiction," God forbid, but by a living truth awful with the sanction of eternal law, the Cross of the Head was, in its glorious merits, the Cross of the member; even as the member's guilt was, in its dreadful demerit, the guilt of the Head. And this is expressed, as a fact not accomplished only but permanent: "There I am (and therefore there He is) still." Not so historically, not so biographically; no, indeed. The Crucified has historically long left the Cross: He has entered for ever into the joy set before Him, having endured. But as to significance and efficacy, the Crucifixion, always and for ever, *is*. *Stat Crux dum volvitur orbis*. Needed every hour, it is every hour a fact. And while it stands, Paul is there, identified with the very Lord of the Atonement, abiding safe indeed with Him.

(c) "Yet I am alive"; alive to God, as we saw just above. "But not I any longer; in me Christ lives." Here is a sentence which on the one hand refuses to be read absolutely and literally; we are quite sure that we must *interpret* as well as read the words. Yet, on the other hand, so deep and also so living is the truth intended, that no exposition can stand which gives to the words a meaning merely conventional and easy. We see at once what the meaning can-*not* be; St. Paul does not mean that his personality was snapped off when he touched Christ, and that he is now literally some one else, or no one personal at all, the subject of a sort of spiritual *nirvana*. I have met with Christians, misled as I cannot but think by partial speculation, who have even eagerly maintained something of that kind; but I am quite sure that St. Paul was not of their school. Every page of his Epistles, notably where he makes allusion to his own experience, is evidence enough to prove his perfect sanity as to the psychology of the new life; in his own view, he is indeed the same person all along. And the sentence immediately before us is enough to secure the point: "Not *I*," true; yet "Christ lives *in me*." The personality is there still, to be the receptable of the Lord.

What then does it mean? We have to remember the immediately preceding clauses.
He has "died to the law"; and *in that respect* "he
no longer lives." He is "dead" in respect to the
hopes, and also to the fears, begotten of himself.
The law has slain the former; and the crucified
Christ the latter. In that respect it is "no
longer I." Paul *is gone*, in the sense of the man
who has hoped for salvation in his own will and
his own works. Paul *is gone*, in the sense of the
man who bears the mortal burthen of the doom
which Christ has borne for him. In both these
respects now "in him Christ lives." The words
express, to the uttermost and the deepest, the
identification of the believer and the Saviour,
alike for the believer's spirtual power and for
his judicial peace. United to Christ, in a
union which can be expressed only as Christ's
indwelling in him, he has the Lord alike for his
peace with God, and for his power for holiness.
It is indeed the Lord; no distant name, radiant
but out of reach as the stars of midnight; no
mere equivalent phrase for the man's own
better self or moral force; no, nothing else nor
less than the personal Christ Himself. Such
is now the treasure hid in this man's human
being. Absolutely beyond our analysis or
definition, yet here is the fact; Christ liveth in
me. I live in Christ; yes, this is divinely true.
But here is the other side of things; alike for

the awful needs of daily life, and for peace before
the white throne of eternal judgment, Christ,
who died for me, *lives in me.*

(d) "Such life as I do now live in flesh (as
regards those grave aspects of the matter in
which I *do* still live, and live under the conditions of earthly life) in faith I live (as if surrounded by faith as my vital air ; for the
watchword now must be, *reliance on Another,*
first, midst, and last) in faith I live, faith resting
on the Son of God, who loved me, and gave
Himself over me."

Pistei te tou uiou tou Theou. The words are of
course, literally, "the faith of the Son of God";
and some have insisted upon rendering them so,
and making the *pistis* to be Christ's fidelity to
His servant. This sense of *pistis* no doubt
exists (see 5. 22, 23). But I venture to say that
that explanation is impossible in the context
here, where the thought of justification, with
our faith in Christ as the receptive act on our
side, has been all along in view.

It is needless to accumulate quotations to
prove the familiar use of *pistis,* "trust," with the
genitive of its Object. What he affirms is that
his life, in all that makes mortal life up, his
life "in the flesh," is lived by trusting the Son
of God. And then, to define and emphasize
that special aspect of this blessed Object of
faith which is mainly present to his thought, he

adds, "Who did love me, and give Himself over
(in atoning death) on my behalf." It is Christ
for me, so appropriated that the eternal love
and the actual salvation are joyfully realized as
"for me." For "us"? Yes. For "the Church"?
Yes. But here, "for me." Nothing less contents this man in his "life in the flesh." Nothing
less than "Christ for me" is his secret for a life
wholly expended on Christ in others.

(e) The closing verse of the passage brings us
back to recollect the original bearing of the
argument. It was the question of righteousness, acceptance, which had occasioned the
dispute at Antioch and had brought out this
wonderful confession of faith. Upon this he
now returns: "I do not nullify the grace of God
(the principle of salvation which makes it a
pure gift from Him, and in no sense a purchase
by me) for if through law is righteousness, then
Christ died for nothing."

But indeed "for nothing" He did *not* die. Not
for an illusory aim, nor when another way
might have been taken, did the Son of God pour
out His soul. And therefore (such is the
sublime logic of the implication) therefore
"righteousness" is mine, through Him given for
me, not through law kept by me. I cast the
ponderous load of *all* my guilt, and of *all* my
weakness, upon Him who loved me. He died
on purpose that I should do this. Not to do so

may wear the mask of humility, but it is to
"stultify the grace of God."

A few detached comments, and I leave this great
passage for that private study of it, and application
of it to life, which will never quite be over.

(*f*) First, note the great spiritual law—death
in order to life.   It is true all round the circle.
Whether we contemplate our safety, or our
holiness, or our happiness, or our strength to
serve God—we must die if we would live.   We
must die to our own dream of merit, if we would
live in the joy of a felt forgiveness.   We must die
to reliance on our self-sanctifying power, if we
would indeed be holy in Christ.   We must die
to our own claims, and surrender absolutely to
Him, if we would taste the one possible perfect
freedom.   We must die to ourselves as our
end and aim, if we would find our true end, life
for others in the Lord.

(*g*) Then let us note what I alluded to above,
the "not I," and "in me."   It has been beautifully
said that the Christian yielded indeed to Christ
and resting on Him, does not cast away his
personal pronoun, but—he inflects it.   "*I*,"
in a deep sense, am annulled; but what a glory
come to "*me*"!   The man abdicates the throne
of his life.   But he does not go out of existence;
he bends himself with reverent joy to be the
throne of his Lord, the habitation of "his King
who has saved him."   More full than ever is the

personality; for it is *inflected* into the abode of Jesus Christ.

(*h*) Lastly, the Christian's life is lived ("in the flesh," under the real conditions of weak, sin-injured, tempted humanity), on the principle of faith in the Son of God. What does this mean? Quite practically—so I would reply— by *making use of* the Son of God. Let me write the phrase with humblest reverence; but so it is. Faith which grasps the Son of God means, translated into the experience of our common days, the reliant use of Him in all He is given to us of God to be. Shall we put the motto into practice? Let our exercise of such faith be duly surrounded and safeguarded indeed with watching, with prayer, and with adoration. But, behind all its safeguards, let it be ever simply this—the making use of Jesus Christ, as He is ours in the covenant of God; our Sacrifice of perfect peace, availing for ever; our Life, indwelling, able to conquer all our enemies within us, making us, now and here, more than conquerors. Let us use Him so, in the hour of subtlest or of fiercest temptation. Then at length we shall use Him as our Redemption from the power of the grave, our Life Eternal; for "he that believeth in Me shall never see death, shall never die."

One further passage only, out of many which invite, I present for notice here.

v. 16, 17. "Now I say, By the Spirit walk, and desire of flesh you shall surely not fulfil. For the flesh desires against the Spirit, and the Spirit against the flesh; for these are each other's opposites; in order to your doing not the things which you choose."

(a) Here first it is manifest that the "Spirit" is not the spirit of man but the Spirit of God; the frequent previous allusions of the Epistle to the "Spirit," as well as the drift of this context, assures us that the word means the Divine Spirit indwelling in the Christian, who has "received the promise of the Spirit by faith." Again, the word "flesh" here is obviously not the mere corporeal frame; no careful reader of St. Paul can think that. Among "the works of the flesh," just below, we find not only fornications and revellings but rivalries and jealousies. No better *practical and popular* equivalent for such "flesh" is to be found than the familiar word "self." "The flesh" is that in man which lies apart from God as its centre and its law.

(b) Here, if I understand him aright, the Apostle implies the grave and humbling fact that always and to the last, yea, "in them that be regenerated," the "flesh" is *there*. Never is it so gone that the believer can dare to say, "There is no mischief latent *in* me; I have only now to think of evils *around* me." This whole context assumes the opposite.

But then—what is the main purpose of the passage? Is it simply, or chiefly, to tell us this? Is it merely to keep us low, and to give us an antidote to perfectionist error? By no means. As we look more closely, we see that the Apostle's leading thought is precisely in the opposite direction. He does indeed remind the Galatians (who were evidently beginning fast to degenerate in their spiritual tempers as well as in their spiritual creed) that the "flesh" was there, and that "in their flesh dwelt no good thing." But he speaks of this only the more to remind them that, as surely as they were Christ's, the Spirit of God dwelt in them, and that in that divine Presence and Power lay a glorious possibility for them; the possibility, not remote but immediate, of their being enabled to say "no" to the bent and gravitation of self, a "no" which should not be only a weary sigh but rather the strong watchword of a soul set free in God.

It is all-important, if we would rightly appreciate the passage, to remember this. At first sight it seems only to warn. It draws the picture of our inner world, and behold, two antagonists are there, watching each other, seeking to thwart each other's action, so that there is a perpetual counteraction going on, under the eye of the *Ego*. But then we look closer, and we see that while one of those antagonists is the all-too-powerful and subtle thing called Self, the other is no less than the Spirit of the living God, able to make the Son of God a conquering reality within the heart, as the man casts his needy being upon the Spirit's side, and gives himself up to be "led by Him."

It was so in Galatia. It is so at this hour all over Christendom, from the oldest Christian Church to the newest mission on the Victoria Lake. It is so in our midst to-day. By the grace of God it may be and shall be so in our hearts, as we too "live our life in the flesh by faith in the Son of God," and remember that deep within us, "lusting against the flesh," so that we may not go its way, is none other than the Eternal Spirit.

NOTES

NOTES

NOTES